# The Discontinuity at the Waistline:

## My #Metoo Poems

Marion Deutsche Cohen

**Rhythm & Bones Press**
Trauma-turned-Art

Rhythm & Bones Press
Birdsboro, Pennsylvania

*The Discontinuity at the Waistline: My #MeToo Poems*
© 2019 Marion Deutsche Cohen
© 2019 Rhythm & Bones Press

Interior Design: Tianna G. Hansen, *Rhythm & Bones Press*
Cover Image: Devin Asher Cohen
ISBN: 978-0-9980432-7-2

Printed by *Ingram Spark, Inc.,* USA
First Edition July 2019

All rights reserved. No part of this book may be reproduced, stored in a retrieval system, or transmitted in any form or by any means, electrical or mechanical, including photocopying, scanning, recording, or posting on the internet, without the written consent of the author, artist, or publisher, with the exception of short excerpts quoted in articles or reviews.

Please note this work and content deals in many ways with sexual assault and trauma. We ask that you take extra care while reading.

rhythmnbone.com/discontinuity-at-the-waistline

# Introduction

*The Discontinuity at the Waistline: My #MeToo Poems* by Marion Deutsche Cohen is a collection of poems focusing on everyday micro-aggressions many women face throughout their lives, from pre-adolescence to adulthood. Wonderful in the way it details the author's early experiences using images from childhood and dreams, transitioning into becoming a married woman and a mother, and depicting her strength and bravery as a woman, this collection sheds light on many realities of women in this world and their stories which are necessary and important to share.

An early review by Beth O'Brien of *Mad Hatter Reviews* states, "Throughout the collection, the description of unwanted male attention and the ability to politely say no without damaging a man's ego are demonstrated with great accuracy. Moreover, Cohen highlights the sexual expectations women often feel compelled to conform to, both in and out of relationships...

Ultimately, this collection is a hard-hitting read but overwhelmingly necessary. Cohen states at the end of the collection, 'I have never been raped or assaulted but there were things I didn't want to do'. Through her poetry Cohen validates the feelings and concerns of her younger self who is surely not alone in these experiences."

By validating what she herself experienced from such a young age, Cohen also validates the experiences of all women who have ever felt uncomfortable in the presence of a man or under expectation from society. We live in a world where culture defines much of the way we act, and this is a subject that Cohen hones on with resilience, unafraid to look at these issues in the face and speak for all those who are still remaining silent. This book highlights all the ways the author is able to eagerly echo the battle cry that so many woman and assault survivors have taken up with, "Me Too!" and gives reason for the reader to journey with her as she travels back, examining everything from her dreams to her sexual habits which are shaped by growing up in a society that has unrealistic and often absurd expectations of what it means to be a woman.

~ Tianna G. Hansen
*Editor-in-Chief*
*Rhythm & Bones Press*

# Advanced Praise for *Discontinuity at the Waistline*

"…this collection is extremely relevant and unfortunately relatable. Of course, it deals with hard-hitting topics, which naturally leave the reader feeling uncomfortable. But from beginning to end, Cohen demonstrates the ability to move between wonderful imagery and cutting clarity in a way that really makes the reader sit up and pay attention.… Cohen's collection is powerful and empowering. By putting these experiences into words, she allows other girls and women to see they are not the only ones who have felt this way, and ultimately that they should not have to feel this way."

~ Beth O'Brien, *Mad Hatter Reviews*

## Praise for Cohen's Previous Work

*for "The Project of Being Alive":*

"There is a great precision and correctness in Marion Cohen's work... We live in a state of shared alone-ness, and this is a book to keep at our bedside and, while reading by oneself, not be alone at all."
-- Mike Cohen, author of "Between the I's" and host of Poetry Aloud and Alive at the Big Blue Marble Bookstore

"I savored her bounty of questions and absence of judgment -- and her sense of astonishment."
-- Rachel Simon, author of "Riding the Bus with My Sister" and "Building a Home with My Husband"

"... Time becomes a network for identity rather than nostalgia. Reality is always being tested..."
-- Hal Sirowitz, author of "Mother Said" (Crown)

\*\*\*

*for "Crossing the Equal Sign":*

"Highly original."
-- Anne Hudson, poetry editor of Facets

"Marion is one of the few poets who can successfully explore the join between the literary and the mathematical sensibilities, and no one does it as well as she."
-- Jet Foncannon, Professor Emeritus, Drexel University

*The Discontinuity at the Waistline:*

*My #MeToo Poems*

# In Their Progressive Household

My father lounged in the bathtub
all smug and squashed.
It was supposed to be cute.
We had all been corralled
into that little room
and there he beached
a great white whale.
His neck a rotten tree trunk
his belly a slimy desert
and *it* like the fat on lamb chops
or a giant toadstool
or a leg of one
of my wobbly rubber dolls.
My sister sat on the toilet
and laughed as he suddenly splashed
and our mother smiled by the sink
in nervous satisfaction.
But I stayed close to the door
not really looking
eyes, in fact, raised
maybe even closed.
I don't remember whether that door was open
don't know how wide the crack
but one hand was near it
the other on the knob.
Mostly, I *remember* that door
how I put-my-right-hand-out
my-left-hand-out.
I was trying to put-
-my-whole-self-out
was positioned to turn and flee.

## Basic Rapist Dream, Pre-adolescent

He would be a few feet before me.
And then he would be upon me.
With very little fuss he would clamp
just under, and in, my armpits
then specifically between my ribs.
And he would lift straight up
he would keep lifting
keep clamping, he would hold his dig.
I would dangle like a baby
frozen, locked
would stiffen like a nerve
fear-itself.
He would flick his Bic, tweedle his dee.
A centipede would crawl onto my heart.
"What lies in Room One-oh-one"
is beyond drama, beyond trauma, beyond your wildest sizzlings.
It's the dead-center root of your birth, your conception.
It's the little egg that couldn't.
It's a mouth held open
for an ocean
an eye held open
for a scoop.
It's Deep Throat, Deep Windpipe.
You on the rocks, you under glass.
It is the Tingler
that slithery metallic lizard
crazily ruthlessly bent
in the middle of its resolve.
"In your case it's" rapists --
well, anything that tingles
anything that clutches and clamps.
The people I called for help
would be more rapists.
And the time that passed
would not heal.
Like a slave on the run I would gasp for North.
But South would be land, South would be sea.
South would be all there was.

South would be the rule.
South would be the exception.
South would be the sky.
South would have won.

## Hope Still Hope

My mother said She's dear to somebody
about the pregnant woman passing us on the sidewalk.
How can she get pregnant without any arms? we had asked.
And decades later I hope
still hope
that what my mother said
was correct.

# Thirteen on the Bus
1956

(1)
An old man sat to my left and told me I was the only one who understood him. Soon he asked to hold my hand and I let him. I kept listening as he kept talking. A woman passenger walked over and whispered to me, "change your seat" and I didn't. That evening my father told me the superintendent of schools' daughter had been killed by such a man.

But I really believed that man was telling me his deepest thoughts. I really believed his deepest thoughts were deep. I really believed he could see, by my facial expression, that here, finally, was someone who Knew. I really believed there was something special about me this man could detect.

And why couldn't anyone else?


(2)
Another man started talking to me and he made it come up, would I marry a Black man (I wasn't Black)? I answered yes and the man thought that meant I'd get off the bus with him

even though he wasn't Black.

# A Page of Short Coming-of-Age Poems

### (1) Fifteen

In our health class question box somebody wrote "Could you tell me, I really want to know, what does sexual intercourse feel like?" But Mrs. Hiller answered only "All I can say is, it's different for everybody. Each couple figures out its own way."

But what were some examples of ways? What did these ways feel like? How many ways were there? Why only one way for each couple? What was her and her husband's way?

### (2) First Thumping, Tenth Grade

I didn't know what it was, before the beginning of Chorus class, about the tall meaty guys in the base section, singing and harmonizing "So Fine" and "Don't Know Why I / Love You Like I Do". Didn't get why all the girls, including me, swooned, or what that thumping was or where in my body it thumped. No, I didn't know. Not yet.

### (3) Fourteen through Sixteen

I didn't get asked out on dates.
Meeting a boy at a party and dancing with him all evening didn't count.
I wanted him to call me up and say Would you like to go to a movie?
Or out for pizza.
Or to another party, a brand new party, not a party we met at but one he'd taken me to.

And, fourteen through sixteen
he didn't.

### (4) Sixteen

All I wanted that I didn't have was to fall and be in love, and all I needed to get that was one boy ask me out, on our date I'd say such wonderful things that, first, he'd fall in love with me and, second, the wonderful things I'd say would cause him to be just like me so I'd fall in love with him and that would settle it, forever and ever. To put your arms around someone who's putting his arms around you and you're in love -- ecstasy, nothing but ecstasy, if only one boy would ask me out.

# Sour Sixteen

### (1) Teenage Weekend

Who arranged this I had no idea but there I suddenly was, the only girl in the car, somebody had decided that those two boys, probably named Pete and Mike, would get me to the dance while Seena and Diane went with the rest of the group. And somebody had put me in the middle of that front seat between those two very fat very loud boys. I hadn't yet had a date nor talked very much to boys. Pete and Mike did all the talking, over and around and through me, the kind of stuff boys talked about, weird stuff, scary stuff, stuff I didn't know much about except to shake in the dress my mother had picked out. There was nothing else to listen to and nowhere else to look. Would we ever get to that dance and what to do when we did, how would I get back home or to school on Monday? Is that what weekends would be like from now on, going back and forth between crowded car rides and crowded dance floors? Those boys didn't rape me but something did.

### (2) Ritchie

My high school friends knew I wanted a real date so they fixed me up, we'd go to the beach and they'd bring along Ritchie, Ritchie Schwartz they said so very likely Jewish and that was supposed to be good though I didn't care and neither did my parents. So we got to the beach and Ritchie had oily blonde hair and a thin scrunchy face and he didn't do math or music but he liked me, liked me a lot, I didn't know what to do. He put his arm around me, I didn't know what to do, he wasn't the real date I wanted, he said What would you do if I kissed you? and I said I'd scream, sort of flirty I guessed, I didn't know what to say. I want to hear you scream he said and I turned away from him quickly, jerkily, that's all I knew to do but he kept his arm around me and I didn't know what else to do.

And then someone had on a radio and there was news of integration vs. segregation and Ritchie said Kill 'em all. Kill who all? I asked and Ritchie said the N-word in the plural and I said No, I don't believe in that, I knew to say that and he said Well that's just one of the ways we differ.

I got home safely without being kissed by Ritchie but I knew he'd call, he really liked me, I didn't know what to do so I asked my mother and she said Just tell him a little white lie, say your parents won't let you date anyone who isn't Jewish

'cause it turned out Ritchie Schwartz wasn't Jewish, I forget how I knew that but thank Goodness, and Ritchie did call and I said what my mother had told me and he quietly murmured Oh. I was giving up a real date, maybe a whole sequence of dates but thank Goodness.

## In Their Progressive Household #2

It was a *short* hallway.
As short as a birth canal.
My father stood at the living room end with a towel around his middle.
And he began to slowly lose the towel.
Not in a sexy way.
Or not that I, at that pre-sex age, would have noticed.
He pulled the towel horizontally
perpendicular to his standing
and when he was finished, what was revealed was a "mere" bathing suit.

But I didn't like looking at his middle.
So I basically didn't.
And my mother?
She, with me, was at the kitchen end of that too-short hallway.
She was wearing her usual housedress.
She never sported her middle.
Never walked around in a bathing suit.
Oh, my sister and I knew she *had* a middle.
She had a body, not only head, hands, and feet.
But we never saw it.
Not even under a towel.


## Statement

I wanted to be introduced to sex by someone I would love forever.
In particular, I didn't want to see any other man's naked middle.
That's why I looked at my father's with mere peripheral vision.
That's why I stayed in the boundaries of those scenes.
That's why, in their progressive household, I wasn't very progressive.
That wasn't the kind of progress
I wanted to make.

**Seventeen and a Quarter**

I didn't want to kiss Conrad.
I didn't like those cold slippery lips.
I didn't know I wasn't in love.
He should not have been my first kiss.
Once he took me to a concert and then while he was kissing me goodnight I
    began humming that Beethoven.
"Hey, you're singing again," he said.
Like, you're crying again.
The trees were swaying and the porch steps were still.
The moon was somewhere in between.

# A Page of First Husband-to-Be Poems

### (1) He Didn't Wait Long Enough

We were on our third date, one of the very-late 50's drive-ins, and he started to kiss me, different from a good-night kiss. I liked him but turned my head. "I just broke up with someone I couldn't stand to kiss so my natural tendency..." something like that.

He listened. He understood. And he stayed still, for about five minutes. Then he started kissing me again. I wanted to keep dating him so I kissed him back, different from a good night kiss. But I didn't want to. It was a few more dates before I wanted to. Just not yet. Not yet.

### (2) His Hands

My mother said "he could put them on your face."
But he'd been putting them on my face for months and now he wanted to put them someplace lower, if I didn't let him he wouldn't know where to put them, that's what he said and I told my mother and she had that suggestion.

Yes, he could just keep putting them on my face. And running them through my hair. Sigh.

### (3) Seduction Culture 1960

He told me his fraternity brothers always talked about what they did to women, how many virgins they broke, one guy said he told this girl he loved her and would she marry him? and after he broke her she excitedly said "ooo, I'm gonna go call my mother and tell her I'm engaged, she'll be so happy" and he answered "don't bother", he bragged about that

and my first husband-to-be was afraid if he told me he loved me, if he said those three mini-words, it would seem like he was just trying to get me to let him break me so he didn't, not for close to a year and when you're in not quite requited love a year is a long time.

## Gone for Hours

When Holly was eight or nine a boy from her neighborhood, big and burly, whispered to her, "Come with me, I want to show you something." They went behind some building or between buildings and first thing he did was take off her underpants. She screamed, kept screaming, she saw neighbors looking out their windows but nobody did anything. And she still doesn't know the second or third thing he did, all she knows is, after all the things he did she was walking home, into her building, through the doorway, inside the kitchen, her mother asked Where WERE you? You've been gone for hours.

Holly didn't know where she'd been and she also didn't know she'd been gone for hours. And ever since then when she hears anybody scream, she goes to investigate, like when she's teaching, her students say "Oh, don't worry about it, they're just fooling around" but she leaves the room, checks the halls, makes sure everything's okay, makes sure if everything isn't okay she'll be somebody who does something.

## Celeb Psychologist

Dr. Albert Ellis gave a talk at my college on "premarital relations", very controversial at the time. "Why buy a pair of shoes without trying them on?" he said.

I thought that was ugly. I wouldn't want to be tried on. Moreover, I had bought shoes that didn't fit. I thought they were pretty and they were half-price.

Maybe just keep in my closet, for decoration. Or out of my closet. Or they'd fit later. Mostly, if you love them they fit in some way.

## College Dating

I met Paul at what they called Visa Dance, meaning foreign students. He was Danish, blond hair, my height, cute puggish nose, and when we found out we both liked classical music we left the dance and went up to the Listening Room on the eighth floor where we listened, just listened. And he asked me out, or rather *in* - he asked me inside his apartment where he'd roast us chestnuts.

My dorm friends warned me about going to a boy's apartment but I didn't say no. First we roasted the chestnuts, then we ate and then we did the dishes. He stood behind me, closer and closer. When the dishes were done he span me around and began. I knew what he was beginning and I span in the other direction. "Relax, girl, relax," he said and that got me even more scared.

I didn't know about saying no but I did, I said I didn't want to, I never had. And he got very tender. He said that wasn't what he'd meant. "But," he said, "I like to touch you." "What do you mean?" I asked. "Like this," he said, placing his hand on my arm and stroking.

And will you believe this? we saw each other every night for a month before I realized it was really the boy back home I loved. Will you believe? all the Danish guy and I did during that month in his apartment was homework, classical music, lie on the couch and sometimes kiss, above the neck. I liked the way he said "litrature" and "Tewish" for "Jewish" and he taught me about "Sehnsucht" from the Schubert Lieder. I left that relationship no less virgin than before. When I think of it now, I think I shouldn't have even kissed him, I should have waited for my first husband, my interim love, or my current.

## That Great Feeling of Safety

When the boy back home finally said those three mini-words I said them too and
then I asked You mean get married and everything?
And he answered Yes.

Not too quickly.
Not too slowly.
And not a Molly Bloom yes.
Not me-just-as-well-as-anybody-else.

And not again and again.
Once, only once.
Once was plenty.
Once was enough.

# Sex 101 (Or: He Meant Well)

My first husband-to-be wanted to take it slowly, spread it over time, minimize my trauma. It was about a two-month course and here was the syllabus: Day One, I touch it, "indirectly" he said, meaning over his thick jeans. It felt silly, what was the pleasure and where was it going? Day Two, he brings it out, centimeter by centimeter, and I touch directly, scared crapless, that skin felt different from other skin. Day Three, I keep touching, learn how to move until he cums. (That was supposed to last us the four years before we could marry.)

And so little by little I learned sex with my first love. Little by little like the poor live lobster someone told me about, the family who bought him was kind, wanted to take it slowly so they plunged it in non-boiling water then turned on the heat 'til the water slowly worked toward a boil.

Two kids under 21, what did we know? In particular, I didn't know that what I wanted was to do it all at once, to yes take it slowly but over two hours, not two months. I wanted one special event, one precious happening, not a sitcom but one glorious movie, all in one super-night ending in one super-morning. And I didn't know that many decades later I would get what I wanted. While taking Sex 101 I didn't know there would be Sex 102, didn't know there was more to the story, if the story's long enough it might have a happy ending.

## Feb. 18, 1961

(1) During, I looked at the ceiling.
After, I looked in the mirror.
In that book the woman had looked in the mirror and asked "Do I look any different?"
No, I didn't look any different.
Or not above the neck.

Ah! but I *felt* different.
Above the neck, too.
That week, on the bus, on the radio... it wasn't even a *dirty* joke, it was a *toilet* joke
I understood toilet jokes better now.
I understood humanity better now.

All of time was divided into before THEN and after THEN.
First breakfast after THEN.
First math class after THEN.
First math test after THEN.

The second time wasn't a THEN.
The hundredth time wasn't a THEN.
There was, during those years
only one THEN.


(2) He had been so gentle.
He had that gentle *look*. It smacked of sad.
It also smacked of horny.
And right now, even happily married to someone else who's gentle
it still kind of does.

## Show and Tell

In NYU undergrad second year I had a urinary tract infection, the kind that hurts. The infirmary doctor had me stand up and show him where it hurt. My clothes were on but where it hurt was too close to my pubic bone. And the way I remember it, he had me show him more than once.

Another doctor, a woman, asked me, in her foreign accent, "You have boyfriend?" I knew what she meant and I was so embarrassed, I answered in one word "Yeswe're engaged". I thought if I didn't give her the totality of information they absolutely wouldn't be able to treat me and I'd be in pain the rest of my life. But I'm glad it wasn't the male doctor I had to tell. I'd rather him see where it hurt than hear about the boyfriend.

## Age about Nineteen

(1) My first-husband-to-be and I had just watched Hiroshima Mon Amour. We were in the car, about to head for my house. And he was so enamored with that movie, it was his first art movie, his first *deep* movie, I expected him to share details about how it made him feel. But instead he leaned over and kissed me, kissed me long, then started petting.

I was disappointed. We were *always* kissing, always petting. Always talking too but at the time just-talking was my druthers.

I was often telling him my druthers but I didn't that time, I just didn't.


(2) He said if I were ever raped he'd still love me but Ginny wouldn't be his very own special Ginny any more.

Well, it wouldn't be MY very own special Ginny any more, either.

But it might be OUR very own special Ginny.

Yes, I think it would.

## Bret-at-14's First Date with Lauren-at-14

First they had to practice. Every ten minutes they had to practice.
Practice talking about books, practice talking about clothes.
Practice him call her up, practice her call him up.
Practice him call her with Henry around, practice her call him with Emily around.
They practiced meeting accidentally, practiced meeting purposely.
There could not be anything they hadn't practiced.

And then, at the end of that week...
well, you know how performances go when you've over-practiced
how everything backs up, how the air gets divided into little black squares.

But they sure did practice
ya gotta admit
they sure did get
in a lot of practice.

## Statements, 2019

(1) Mary believes too much is being made about #Metoo. She says she doesn't think what Al Franken did was so bad. The women should get over it, she says. They've been helicopter-parented, over-protected, raised to be fragile, weak, underpowered, she's so glad she wasn't raised that way. "Get over it," she keeps repeating.

I'm someone who gets over things. Mary says losing a newborn baby is a lot worse than being raped. Well, losing a newborn baby is a lot *like* being raped. Your body has been used as an instrument of death. Also, the caregiving part of spousal chronic illness, especially toileting, is a lot like being raped. It involves bodies, bodies that don't want to be touched in that way.

I told Mary I got over it, got over *them*, in the sense that they didn't ruin my life nor give me a bad case of PTSD. I had further babies, got a new love, I *sought* further babies, *sought* a new love.

But, I said to Mary, I bemoan how society views sex. We're a rape culture, assault culture, seduction culture, harassment culture, sexist culture, oversexed culture. Mary says that's changing. Later she said she *hopes* it's changing.

I did both, got over what happened to me and made too much of it. Meaning I made enough of it. And those things shouldn't have happened. And our culture shouldn't have made them worse.


(2) Mary said a long time ago she was in the office alone with her boss. He was sitting at his desk and she was standing up and all of a sudden he blurted out "I'd like to fuck you."

She says she wasn't upset, she simply told him "not gonna happen". And after that, she says, he never mentioned it again and she advanced in the job, no problem.

None of that #Metoo stuff.

Not that time.

# A Page of Dreams

### (1) Former-Well-Spouse Post-Traumatic

I'm caregiving a fat man, lifting him from bed to wheelchair. The only way I can keep my arms around him is to lock my fingers together. And now I can't unlock them. There's no leverage, no wriggle room. I'll be handcuffed here forever, forced around my care receiver, hands too far from my face, nose against his suffocating stomach. I decide to struggle without room or leverage. I use whatever might I have. And I guess I have a lot because first come the middle two fingers, then follow the others, all released and happily stretching, waving in coolest air. What a blessing, to be back in the open. What a relief, to have separated hands.

### (2) Total Nightmare

I'm in love with two men, my real-life second husband and somebody new. The new man is tall, dark, handsome, and kind. I love both exactly the same.

Oh, why was I so stupid, to sleep with the new man? On the other hand, why was I so stupid, to be already married?

And now I'm supposed to meet one of them for breakfast and I can't remember which. I also can't remember where. I decide to eat at the first restaurant I find, stand whichever one up while I do some thinking. It's one of those places where all they have is scrambled eggs and toast. At least that's one decision I won't have to make.

### (3) She Marries a Man

She marries a man because he has thirty-two children who need a mother. But when he brings her home... well yes, it's crowded, constant movement, kids and friends of all ages. But each kid is managing just fine. They don't need a mother.

Even when there's a crisis they're still just fine. She checks each one and they all truly are. Her husband is nowhere to be seen. She could leave but it's so nice to be in a house where everybody's managing just fine.

## Temper Tantrums at Home

It's different when a man does it.
A man doesn't rave on and on.
A man simply starts and stops.
A man just goes at it, doesn't go at it *again*.
A man doesn't pause, he ends
and, you can be sure, not with a whimper.
When a man does it it's scolding, not pleading.
When a man does it he's a beast, not a bird.

It's different when a man does it.
A man doesn't stomp his foot and if he did, it would ram through the floor.
A man doesn't throw pots and pans; a man throws chairs, tables, rooms.
A man doesn't hit the ceiling; he raises the roof, dislodges the sky.

His are not the ravings of the powerless.
His are the ravings of the powerful.

It's different when a man does it.
When a man says This is the last straw, you'd better make ready to gulp.
When a man screams Hell, you'd better start saying your prayers.
When a man cries Shit, you'd better run for the potty.
When a man yells Fuck, you'd better start yelling rape.

## Unwanted

(1) I was out on a short errand one early fall evening, the air dark-grey. My three children were with me, ages ten, six, and five months. We were at a corner waiting for the green light and a man stopped, first, to admire the baby, then to ask me whether I'd like to join him in a drink. Before I could say there was a father back home Arin, the six-year-old, piped "Are you gonna MARRY my mom?"

The man seemed a trifle flustered. "Uh... no... not marry. I was just wondering if she'd like to go out for a drink". And as we walked away I didn't yet know the extent to which Arin would continue to try to protect me

the extent to which he would succeed

the extent to which he couldn't.


(2) One of the 70s feminist articles said Never get on an elevator when the only other passenger is a strange man but it didn't say anything about revolving doors.

I didn't get on with that strange man, *he* got on with *me*, I mean in the same sector. He was with a bunch of rowdy men, men not boys. I was in there already and I couldn't get out, the door had already started revolving and it wasn't finished.

He didn't rub up against me but he laughed and his friends laughed too. I didn't laugh. I didn't even smirk.


(3) Omigod, escalators.

## Rom Com

There's a lot to critique, plenty of plotholes, but it was so damn interesting, every minute, every second. Everything every person said was creative, nobody said just-plain hello or just-wait'll-I-tell-you, everything was a topic sentence or punchline, what reviewers call smart and funny.

It was like everybody, not only the main couple, was flirting with everybody else. If real life were like that, if everything everybody said were that smart and funny and flirty, I'd get tired but a movie is a movie so I just lay back in my seat, completely un-smart and un-funny, I let that movie do all the talking, all the flirting, and I didn't have to flirt back.

## The Freud-Totin' Man

My father was a Freud-totin' man, as in "Freud would have a lot to say about that."

"That" was me having crushes on guys not my father and the "lot to say" was the Oedipus Complex, by which my father really meant the Electra complex. Whenever I talked about Joe or Jeff, it seemed like he and Freud were toting, "Deep Down Inside it's really your father you're crushing on."

Twenty five years later my therapist said "Your father sounds like a very scary man." And yes, I was scared.

## Harassment in Academia

Roberta was getting bored teaching Calc and Pre-Calc semester after semester and her department chair said Let's talk about getting some higher-level courses for you. He meant talk about it over dinner.

He came over to her side of the table. "There's going to be a price," he said. Then he came closer.

She stood up, finished the semester teaching Calc and Pre-Calc, then got out of there, had to find someplace else, someplace else to teach Calc and Pre-Calc.

## Some Food for Thought

### (1) Silenced

A friend once told me her husband's brother hit on her. "And I can't for the life of me figure out why I didn't tell my husband," she said.

Indeed.

### (2) Misogynistic Movie

For the sole purpose of having a child, a young woman marries a slightly older guy. She fucks him to death.
The movie compared that woman to a bee.
But a woman doesn't necessarily want only one child.

### (3) Still Life with Recent Dream and Fear

Dream: I'm breastfeeding a baby, something I loved, something I always hope to dream about. But the baby keeps pulling away. "Every time I latch on," he says, "you stop letting out the milk."

Fear: every time my husband latches on (something I love and don't need to dream about), I'll stop feeling horny.

### (4) Really

I was in my mid-twenties, walking along Riverside Drive in New York City, wearing a jumpsuit I'd made, it was three-tiered vertically like a layer cake, wool fabrics in two shades of grey, one of white-ish pink. A young guy passed by, shrugged, hesitated, then said, "That's REALLY a cute outfit."

And I still feel as though he were saying "Really, honestly, I'm not hitting on you, I just HAVE to compliment you, that outfit is so cute."

I feel as though he were apologizing

and as though he had to say really

as opposed to pretend.

# Two More Dreams

### (1) Subtle

A new love says, "Making love is subtle." He says that a few times, slowly, ethereally, echoingly. She can't wait to make love with him, see what his subtleties are. Maybe he'll even undress her. Maybe he'll even undress her slowly.

To make sure, though, she wears an ultra-long dress. It's more than a burka, more than a giant baby bunting, it might even flow down to below the ground. Plus, it has a high neck and long fitted sleeves, he'll *have* to reach behind her, *have* to undo the lone short zipper at the back and then he'll have no choice but to gently pull that length over her head. He'll be forced, she figures, to caress her long hair, graze against every precious square-inch of her, stroke through the material of that dress.

But no, somehow his hand is suddenly at her naked root, there his fingers are, however they got there. "I thought you said subtle," she gasps, a gasp like a scream and as in a nightmare she shakes herself awake, muscles clenching, eyes quickly opening, continuing to lament "subtle, subtle, I thought you said subtle."

### (2) Dream of Assault Before #MeToo
    July 2005

In a small circular conference room, standing and talking in an even smaller circle, I suddenly become aware that one of the men has his hands around my throat.

"Hey, whadder you doing?" "Oh, sorry."

Later, in another small room, I'm reporting the incident. But the person I'm reporting it to says, "You're talking about a man of impeccable character."

"But I'M a WOMAN of impeccable character."

That dream ends with my many lemmas.

It does not end with any big theorem.

## Sex for One

I am in front of myself with horny-ness.
What I really want is my husband
and he is downstairs.
If I called him upstairs he would not do what I'm doing.
He would not know where my spaces are.
He would not spread his fingers in the correct way.
I would have to explain that I like a cloth
between the touched and the touching.
I would have to tell him when to remove the cloth.

If I were to leap from me to him
to translate my self to his self
something would be lost in translation.
Oh, he'd know that I'm a fractal
but he would not know
my precise current shape.

## Bad Clit Day

She just won't.
The way a cat just isn't a lapsitter.
The way a crawling baby won't let you hold her.

*She* made no marriage vows.
*She* made no commitment.
Who knows how faithful she is and when?

Like our toaster, twice
and the printer, three times.
They just wouldn't.
And then they did.

## Famous Math Guy

John Conway of Conway tiles, surreal numbers, and The Game of Life once flirted at me. I was in the lobby about to go in and give one of my presentations, he was standing there with his cohorts waiting to go to lunch. I had on my wedding ring. "Would you like to join us?" he asked. I'd never met him. "You look like a nice woman," he continued. One of my math friends once told me he propositioned her. I say he flirted *at* me not *with* because I didn't flirt back. But when I got home from that Math/Art conference, it was one of the things I told everybody about.

## That Couple in Ross

"Baby, you look great in that, get that." "You look sharp in that too, get that too."

She walks with a cane but he goes over to the rack of black sequined tops. "Here, try on this one. I think you'd look really smashing in this." Then "Oh Baby, yes! Yes! But I think you need the next size. Lemma go get it."

While he's getting it I say to her "I guess you know you really lucked out."

"Yeah," she agrees, "he loves to shop." They're getting married next month, she tells me. I'm sure he'll notice her wedding dress, maybe he'll insist on seeing it beforehand, maybe even pick it out with her.

And sometimes I wish I wasn't a writer-math-Ph.D., maybe I'd've gotten a guy who just-loves to shop and who thinks I'd look great in this and that but I need the next or the previous size and he'll go find it for me.

I say all that to the guy I did get and I add "Oh well, maybe he beats her up and maybe she doesn't love to shop, maybe she loves math and he won't let her do it, maybe she loves current events and he won't let her google anything. Maybe he takes her around every day to every store and brings her every black sequined top and bottom, maybe he takes them home along with her, rips them up, makes her model kinky, the white bridal dress too."

## Almost Raped or Assaulted or Whatever He Intended

On the streets whenever a guy or guys intercepted me, I would scream "Leave me alone", loud, very loud, for all to hear, even if the closest hearer was on the opposite side of the street. And the guy would get scared and take off.

But once, around 9:00 P on a summer evening, I was walking across the Square from facilitating my Math Anxiety Workshop, the guy said "Scream all you want."

But then one of the students from my workshop appeared on and then off his bike. "Take off," he gestured and the guy did.

That student wasn't much taller than me, didn't speak louder than me, maybe wasn't stronger than me. He was simply male. All that student needed do was gesture, maybe simply appear, just like certain machines break down for a woman but when a man tackles them they behave. Her hero. Sometimes, when you're male, you don't have to do much talking, screaming, or trying.

# Escape from Rapist Mountain
   dream about ending therapy, 1988

I am about to
I am perched
and I am looking back

at the boards, the structure
the skeleton of that house
at the mere residue of enemies
one to each thin board
all divided and still
as so many sleeping blackbirds.

I am about to
I am springing
and, now, merely *thinking* back
back to that picture, back to that frame
back, especially, to my unseen companion

who is not about to
who has come with me only this far.
She is small, far behind
and already flitting from board to board.

Kathy, you'll be fine there.
It's not *your* mother's attic.
You'll be quite safe, quite sound
there in your work, your expertise
your life with the enemies of others.

And I
I'll be fine, too.
I'll be very fine.
It will be good, though, to know
that if ever I have to return
there you'll be. In fact, there you'll *have been*
minding the enemies, keeping them sleeping
keeping them divided, keeping them conquered
keeping them tame, declawed and unbreeding

or perhaps only keeping them company.

## Sex for One-and-a-Half

When I was thirty-seven I bought a vibrator at a feminist conference and my first husband bless his soul said in that attentive nurturing way "Listen, do you want to?"

"I'll help you," he continued. "I'll show you how." I don't remember needing to be helped or shown how, or for that matter needing the vibrator. All I remember is laughing happily.

Jeff then said I could any time I wanted but he'd like to be there. And... well, I cheated. A person can be monogamous and still cheat, she can be monogamous and adulterous at the same time.

## Hitting

I remember hitting
so long ago
and not very often.
And not spanking.
Only the quick deciding, the lift of my arm
the flight of my hand, that final sharp curve.
And then the impact
the skin emerged branded.
They did not say That didn't hurt.
It did not hurt me more than it hurt them.

And I remember grabbing
an arm, a wrist, whatever I could get
and holding tight
then swinging fast.
I remember the smart of that bony part.

It wasn't the same body or mind that had slipped
   out of me years before.
All those cells had been replaced.
But it was, for sure, the same miniature hand
which, just that morning, had roamed like a sleepwalker over my face
and the same toy fist which had rolled
like a wound in mud. And the same shoulder
had pressed and flexed. And the same foot
had wriggled and tapped. And the flat of *my* hand
*that* was the same, the bona-fide same
as what, that morning, had pressed and clutched, those cells the same
every one.

Nowadays hitting children is considered child abuse and I agree, it is.
But please don't ostracize me.
Please don't indict me.
Please don't imprison me
for very long.
And please don't fire me
from being a mother.

## Watching Her Molested Child Sleep: A Piece of Flash-Fiction

Sheet, blanket, pajamas, she is suspicious of everything that touches him. These things can't move, she reminds herself, these things can't approach. And now here comes one of the cats.

Freddie can move but he won't rub. If he rubs, he won't rub in that way. If he does he won't tell her child that this is how it's supposed to be, this is what all pets do, to all children, when they come of age. Freddie won't say It will be our little secret. Freddie, in fact, moves and rubs for all to see.

And the mother asks Does that mean he's okay?

## Scared and the Intermediate Value Theorem

On a connected surface
one can always, quite smoothly and without abandoning
get from any one point to any other.
A man's body is connected.
And I've been at hands, lips, shoulders.
So how come there's that discontinuity at the waistline?
How come I can go only halfway?
How come that waistline is throbbing with infinity?
And my hand and heart throbbing
with zero?

## My New Love

In the middle of the night I'm glad
that he understands that sometimes I like to be touching
not him but the air he warms up.
I like to be where I can feel him
but wake him just enough
so he moves, maybe, half an inch
and then maybe I'll move a quarter inch
and he'll move an eighth.

What would Zeno say
to being so near away?
    2002

# I Love

I love to receive him.
And he loves to give him.
And I love to give him back.
And then – greedy me
receive him again.

And I know it's better to give than to receive.
But I can't seem to make up my mind.
And I know Shakespeare said Never a borrower nor a lender be.
But can't I borrow him for just a second
before I lend him back?

## A Big Deal

(1) My mother said You know, once a boy gets excited, you can't backtrack, it's a big deal, you have to keep going, otherwise he'll be in pain.

So I was careful not to get my first husband-to-be excited. But he got excited anyway. First it was We're gonna *hafta* go below the neck, then We're gonna *hafta* go below the waistline, soon We're gonna *hafta* go below the public bone.

And seventeen years later after our third baby died, I'm sorry but you're gonna *hafta* make me cum. It was one week-post-partum, *I* wasn't gonna cum and there was nothing to make me pregnant again, not yet. I wasn't as good at saying no as I am now and I cried the whole time, maybe he did too.

And I spent a lot of our life together hoping he wouldn't get excited when I wasn't.


(2) Is it true? I asked my second husband. Does it really cause the man pain if he starts and doesn't continue?

Nah! he answered.

And a friend of mine asked her male friend the same thing and he also answered Nah.

I asked my second husband what he thinks a man should do if he starts and isn't permitted to continue and he said Just do something else.

I guess my first husband didn't want to do something else.

## 17 Again

I *told* Connie I didn't like kissing, I was *afraid* of kissing, and he said Well, you have to get used to it.

He was 23, I newly 17 and newly dating (newly kissing). We both should have known better but he should have known even better.

And I was the one who knew better first.

## Watching Nicholas Sparks Movies: A Lament

I have been in requited love three times. But we didn't scamper. Or chase each other around trees or splash around in lakes or have our own special nature-like meeting place. And since I'm five-foot-nine – I was never a head shorter than anybody – and although they each could drape one arm across my shoulders, we never strolled that way or not for long.

None of them could trail an arm down the length of me. I haven't ever had the heaven of nuzzling standing up in the crock of anybody's arm or not very deeply and not, again, for very long, I'm a virgin in that way.

And that renders me sorry for myself, sort of makes me want to sob and weep. Maybe I was never really in love. Or *they* weren't really in love. Maybe I never loved or was loved. It certainly felt and feels like love but maybe not. Maybe, Nicholas Sparks, not.

## The Surreal Schlong Dream (or A Tale of Two)

The man's top was above the table and his bottom was below, meaning his bottoms *were* below. I was also below. I was supposed to go down on both, alternating one with the other.

The one on the left was the schlong. The one on the right was kind of a schlort. That one didn't make me gag but the schlong did.

"Hey," I shouted up. "I'm trying but the schlong is making me gag."

"Okay," called down the man, "just concentrate on the other one."

Gee, that was nice of him.

Or that was nice of half of him.

## Growing Old Together

What I'm most afraid of
one of us gets sagging slobbery lips
but still wants to kiss.
Growing old together means letting go
in particular, of each other
simply being side by side, talking, remembering
not planning a future.
In one movie she lamented "All those years... what was the point?"
and he nodded, held her firmly with one arm, "let's take a walk."
So they strolled together
slowly
through a pastel garden that was not theirs.

# Prude

I don't get it, in movies if somebody's angry at somebody else she slaps that else in the face. That means touching the face and that's not only violent, it's intimate, I'd be too shy to slap somebody in the face.

Also, throwing up. When something bad happens the protagonist throws up. I don't get it, why throw up? Why not cry? Or scream? I'd be too shy to throw up in front of an audience but I wouldn't be too shy to cry or scream.

## Saying No

In my adolescence I usually said no when I needed to but that was to sex-things. It took me a lot longer to say no to typing my first husband's physics papers. I didn't really think I should have to, even his friends said Why don't you just HIRE a typist?

When I finally realized I could say no I *did* say no, not only to typing but to nights, lifting, and toilet, meaning at-home caregiving, and no to visiting him at the nursing home once his cognitive loss and paranoia made him verbally and financially abusive, also no to not getting rid of those four plastic turquoise-blue non-deflatable special mattresses because he always wanted to hold on to things just in case.

Well, sometimes we say no and sometimes we don't. And just because we didn't say no at first, just because we didn't say no at second or third or fourth, doesn't mean we can't say no at *last*.

And next-to-last.

And most of the times before that.

## From the Poet to Her Beloved

Don't creep up behind me while I'm working.
Don't tenderly kiss my hair.
Don't write I love you in the margin.
Don't stand in the doorway and watch with interest or pride.
Don't say let me know when I can speak.
Don't walk in beauty like the night.
Don't try to be my muse.

## The Thing about Men (meant in good spirit)

What is it with men? they always wake up. My first husband woke up almost before he fell asleep and at the slightest cuddle he'd go "touch Henry" and I'd have to, then he'd use that as an excuse to get horny. Men are always waking up.

My second husband isn't like that. He sleeps through the night, cuddles through the night too, actively cuddles without getting horny. But in the morning if he's still asleep, and he usually is, I like to get behind him, my front to his back but then he turns around. Men always turn around.

If I merely look at him he still turns around. This isn't unwanted *sexual* activity but it is unwanted activity. Men are too active. They can't stay put. What is it with men, always so frisky? Do they have to be asleep in order to lie still? Do they have to move in order to breathe? Whatsamatter with men? They're like children, should be seen but not heard, they're like women, should calm down, just relax, don't be so nervous, don't get so mental, don't get so hysterical.

**Not Saying No**

I have never been raped or assaulted but there were things I didn't want to do:
see my father naked in the hallway
hear all those dirty jokes I didn't get
kiss Conrad
kiss/pet with my first fiancé because he had decided it was time to.

And in the 70s at a Second Wave Radical Feminist event, Kathy Fire
   came up from behind me and began massaging my shoulders. I didn't say no
   because I didn't want to be a bad Sister.

And my first husband when he had end-stage M.S., it took him hours to cum and
   he kept trying.

But age 59, single again and falling in love again, I had learned to not do
   what I didn't want. And *he* had learned to not do what I didn't want.

Still, when I put out my tongue, was that specifically so I'd beat him to the punch?
   I think very probably not but still. Not quite sure. Not quite sure.

## ACKNOWLEDGEMENTS

"In Their Progressive Household" appeared in The Screech Owl.
"He Didn't Wait Long Enough" appeared in the anthology "Philadelphia Says Me-Too".
'Seventeen and a Quarter" appeared in Silver Birch Press.
"Seduction Culture 1960" appeared in Hamline Lit.
"Sex for One" appeared in Feckless Cunt.
"Bad Clit Day" appeared in Tawdry Bawdry.
"Scared and the Intermediate Value Theorem" appeared in Strange Attractors: Poems of Love and Mathematics (AKPeters, eds. Glaz and Growney).

## ABOUT THE AUTHOR

Marion Deutsche Cohen is the author of 27 collections of poetry or memoir; her two latest poetry collections are "The Project of Being Alive" (New Plains Press, AL) and "New Heights in Non-Structure" (dancing girl press, IL), about home-schooling and other ideas about engaging with children. She is also the author of two controversial memoirs about spousal chronic illness, a trilogy diary of late-pregnancy loss, and of "Crossing the Equal Sign", about the experience of mathematics. She teaches a course she developed, "Mathematics in Literature" at Arcadia and at Drexel Universities. A poetry chapbook, "Truth and Beauty", about the interaction in that course among students and teacher, was released in 2016 from WordTech Editions. Other interests are classical piano, singing, Scrabble, thrift-shopping, four grown children, and five grands. About this current book she says, "I've never been raped or assaulted, but I still say #metoo b/c I have experienced, in the words of Larry Robin of Moonstone Arts in Philadelphia, 'unwanted sexual activity'. This book is mostly about micro-aggressions (which don't always feel all that micro). We live in a rape culture, assault culture, harassment culture, oversexed culture." Marion's website is marioncohen.net.

## ABOUT THE COVER ART

The Gurgie on the cover is the cutest stuffed animal in the world, or so think the author and the cover-artist, Devin Cohen. The actual Gurgie stands several inches tall, and was obtained from a thrift store by the author and given to her son the artist. Devin was then a child under ten, and Gurgie was loved by everyone in the household. The author, artist, and publishers agree that Gurgie is an apt symbol of gentle-ness and sweet-ness, which is one of the important messages that the book is meant to convey.

## ABOUT THE PRESS

**Rhythm & Bones Press** is a small independent press from Pennsylvania dedicated to highlighting dynamic and inspirational authors whose work deserves to be acknowledged. They specialize in authors who write with personal emotion and those with trauma to portray to the world. They aim to help turn Trauma into Art. Visit them at *rhythmnbone.com* for more information, to find more of their books, or to check out their online quarterly literary magazine and Necropolis blog. Find them on Twitter/FB @RhythmBonesLit or Instagram @RhythmBonesPress. Be sure to find them on GoodReads and rate this book!

# More by Rhythm & Bones Press

*You Are Not Your Rape* anthology

*Lady Saturn* – Wanda Deglane

*Puritan U* – Kristin Garth

*The saint of milk and flames* – Kate Garrett

*Flowers of the Flesh* – Effy Winter

*A Victorian Dollhousing Ceremony* – Tianna G. Hansen, Kristin Garth, Justin Karcher

# Coming Soon

*Was it R\*pe* – Elisabeth Horan
(August 2019)

*at the water's edge* – Nadia Gerassimenko
(September 2019)

*A Very Thin Line* – Rohan Sharma
(November 2019)

www.ingramcontent.com/pod-product-compliance
Lightning Source LLC
Chambersburg PA
CBHW070440010526
44118CB00014B/2133